Acknowledgements
The author, photographer and publisher would like to thank Dr Shanti Kanungo of Cuttack, Orissa, without whose help this book would not have been possible.

British Library Cataloguing in Publication Data

Mathieson, Feroza
Lost at the fair.
I. Title II. Das, Prodeepta III. Series
823'.914[J]

ISBN 0–7136–3065–5

Published by A & C Black (Publishers) Ltd
35 Bedford Row, London WC1R 4JH

Filmset by August Filmsetting, Haydock, St Helens
Printed in Belgium by Henri Proost and Cie Pvba

Lost at the Fair

Feroza Mathieson
Photographs by Prodeepta Das

A & C Black · London

It was Saturday afternoon and Rama arrived at Jivan's house. He was taking Jivan to the fair which came to town once a year.

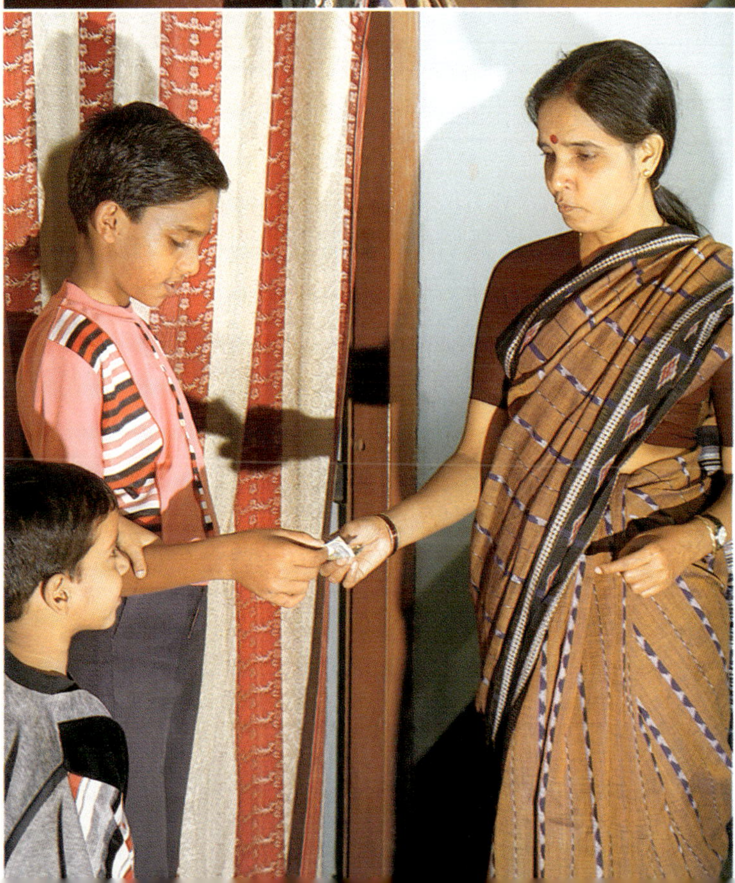

'Now Jivan,' said his mum. 'You be a good boy and stay with Rama. Don't go wandering off by yourself.'

She gave Rama some money which he put safely in his pocket.

'Have a nice time,' called Mum.
'And remember, stay with Rama.'

Soon they arrived at the fairground. What a sight!

There were all kinds of different stalls and rides, even games where you could win prizes if you were lucky.

'Look at that!' said Jivan.

There in front of them was a great big wheel.

'Can we have a go? Please, please!' said Jivan excitedly, and he pulled Rama towards the long queue.

It was worth waiting for a turn. From the top of the wheel, you could see everything.

Jivan wanted to go on the wheel again and again, but Rama decided that three rides were quite enough.

After the ride, they had a look round.

They saw a bird sitting on a swing. It was very clever. It sang a song and did tricks at the same time, all without falling off. Jivan wanted to take it home.

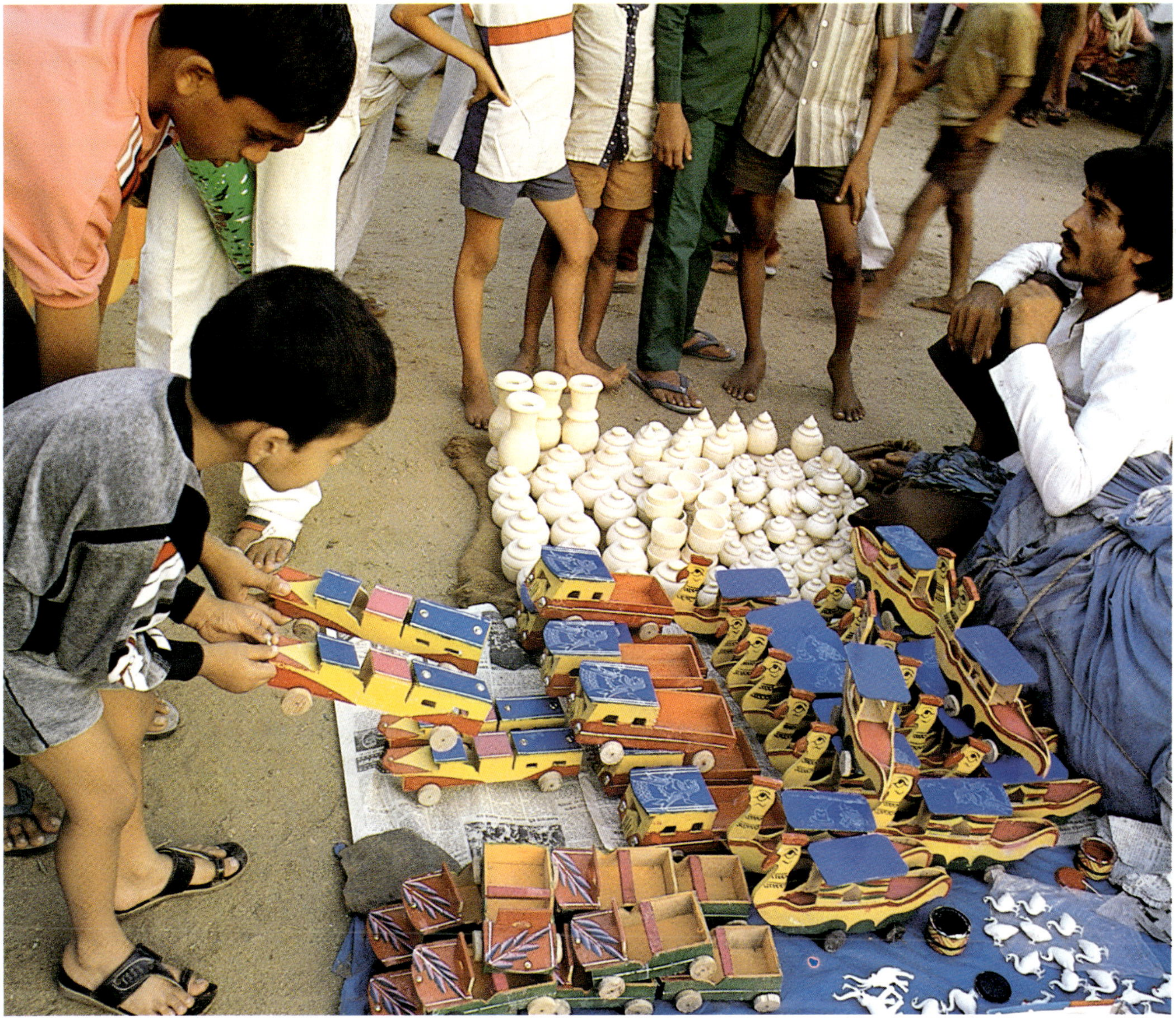

They had a look at all the toys for sale, but Jivan couldn't decide which one to buy.

'Flutes for sale, flutes for sale.'

Jivan and Rama saw a man with lots of flutes on the end of a long stick. Rama tried one out, but they decided not to buy it.

‘What about a balloon?’ said Rama. Jivan didn’t know what to spend his money on.

In the end, they decided on an ice-cream.

‘Let’s have a ride on the aeroplane,’ said Jivan.

‘All right,’ said Rama. ‘Then we must go home. It will be dark soon.’

But when the ride was over, Jivan didn’t want to go. ‘Just one more ride,’ he said. ‘Come on Rama.’

Then they had a go at shooting. 'You might win a prize.' said Jivan. But they didn't win any prizes.

‘That’s enough. It’s time to go home,’ said Rama.

‘Not just yet,’ said Jivan. ‘I want to try on a mask.’
He hurried over to the stall. ‘Look, Rama. I’m Ganesh.’

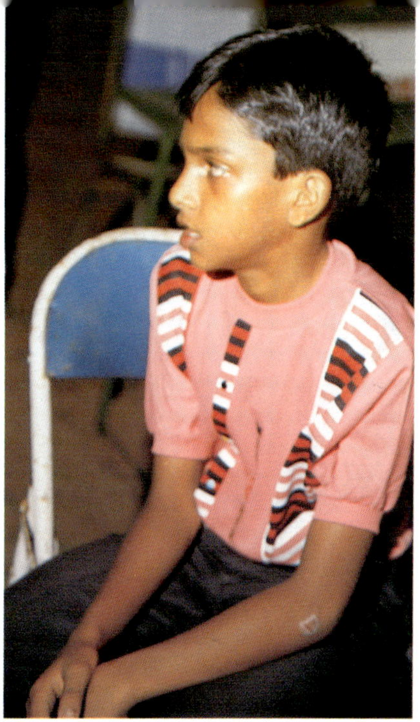

It got darker and darker. Rama was worried. His mum would be wondering where he was.

'Let's buy some sweets,' said Jivan.

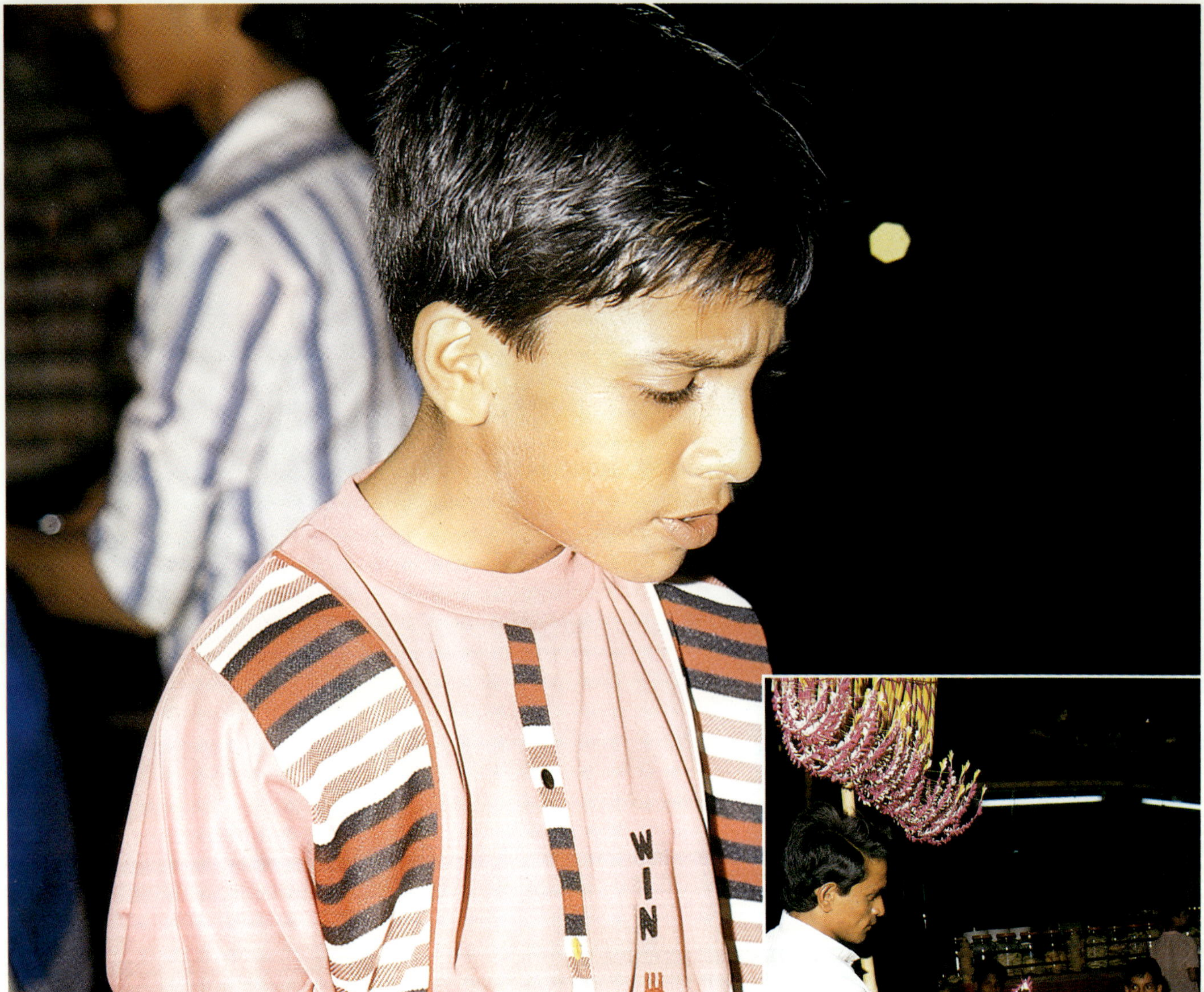

Rama was getting cross. 'Come on, it's time to go home,' he said again.

'I've still got some money left,' said Jivan. 'Watch me try this bow and arrow.' When he had finished, he wanted a go on the roundabout.

'You can stay here by yourself if you want to, I'm going home,' said Rama. And he began to walk away.

'I can have more fun by myself, anyway,' thought Jivan.

He had a go on the roundabout.

He looked at the model cars,
but he didn't buy one.

He bought himself some chat
to eat.

But it wasn't much fun by himself.

Suddenly, Jivan noticed how dark it was.

He looked in his pocket and found he didn't have enough money to get home.

Poor Jivan. What was he going to do now? He didn't want to walk home by himself in the dark. He didn't even know the way home.

Then he spotted Rama. Thank goodness.
'He must have been hiding to frighten me,'
thought Jivan. He waved as hard as he could.

But it wasn't Rama after all. It was someone else.
Jivan really was by himself, all alone in the dark.

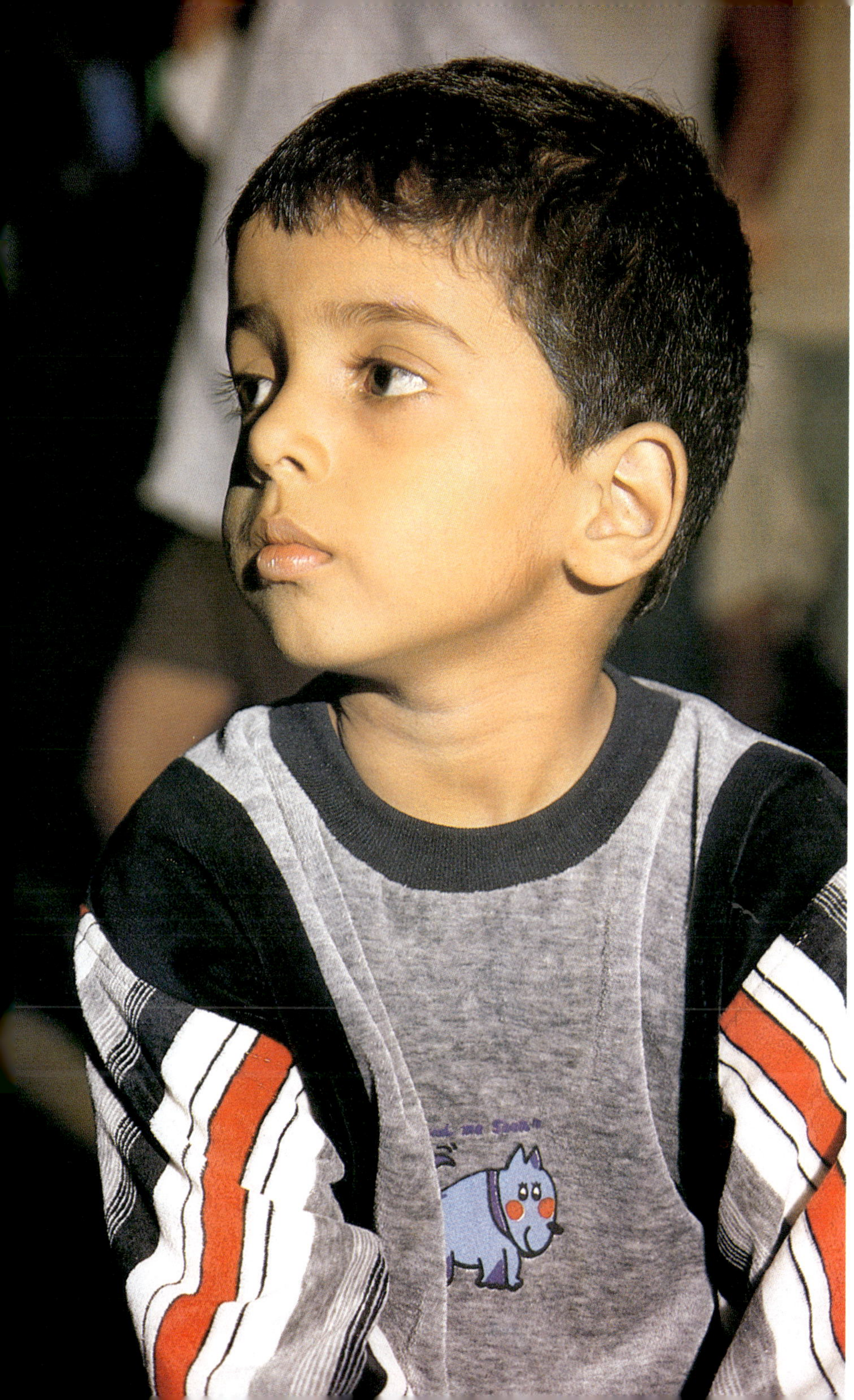

Jivan began to cry. But just then, he heard someone calling his name. Who do you think it was?

Yes, it was Rama. He had come back to take Jivan home safely. Jivan was so pleased to see him that he gave Rama a big hug. 'I'm sorry,' he said. 'I should have done what you told me.'

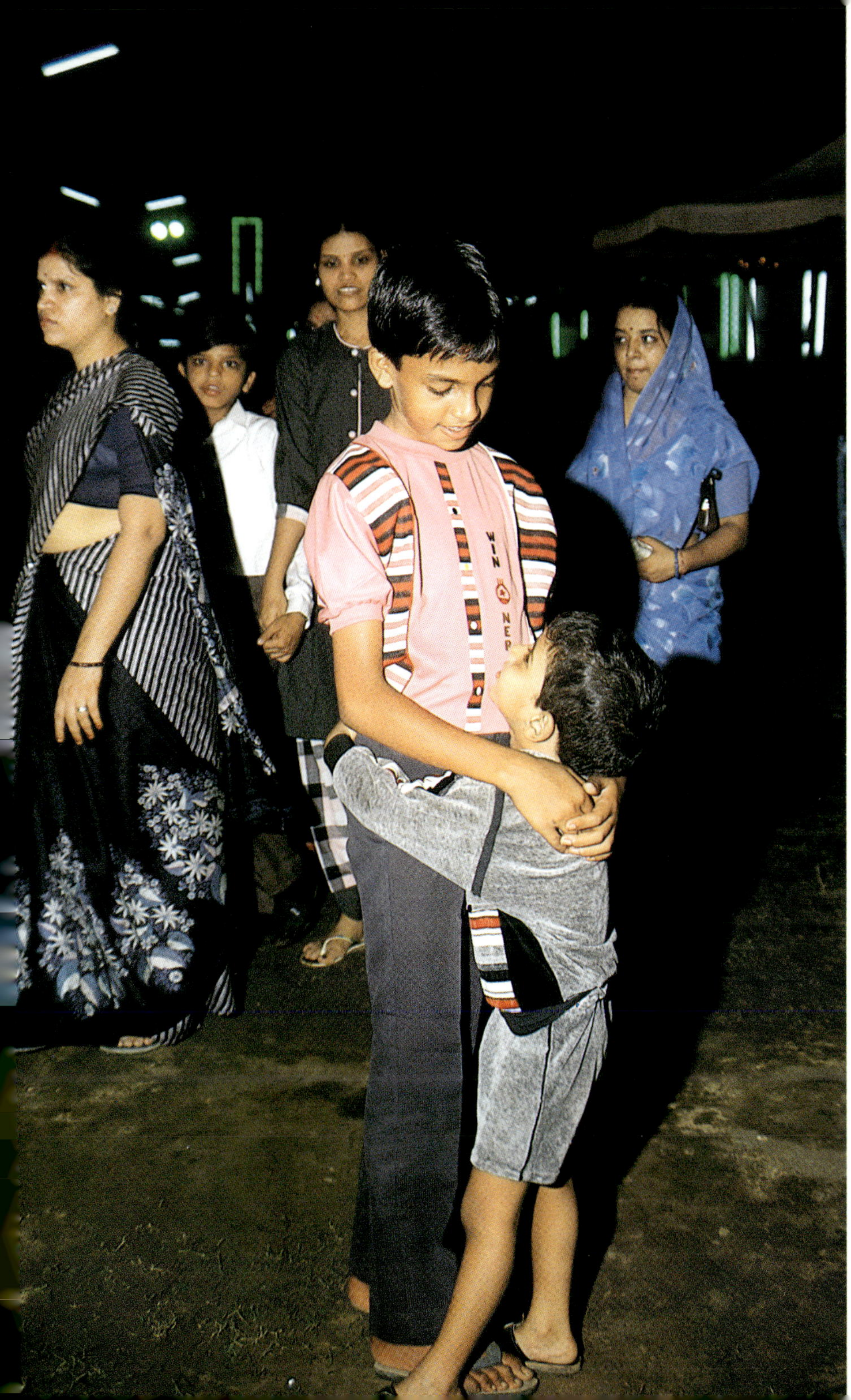

'Never mind,'
said Rama.
'Let's go home.'

'Yes, let's go
home,' agreed Jivan.
'I've had enough
of the fair.'